Texting with...

Women's History

Amelia Earhart - Harriet Tubman - Cleopatra

Written by Bobby Basil

This is a work of creative nonfiction. It is inspired by the life of the subject. It is not an encyclopedic account of events and accomplishments of the subject's life.

3 FREE BOOKS!

Go to historytexting.com!

Hi! I'm Alex!

I’m nine, and I don't know
what I want to be
when I grow up.

There are so many
amazing things to do!

My mom helps me text with
important people and ask them
questions about their lives.

It's fun to ask questions!

Today
my mom and I are
texting with...

Amelia Earhart!

Amelia Earhart was an
American aviation pioneer
that lived from 1897 until 1937.

She was the first woman
to fly solo across
the Atlantic Ocean.

I can't wait to text her
my questions!

Hi Amelia!

Hi Alex!

Thank you for texting with me.

You're welcome.

What do you look like?

I look like this...

Where were you born?

I was born in Atchison, Kansas.

What was your childhood like?

Growing up, I was very close to my sister. I called her Pidge.

I've never heard that name before!

It's a nickname. Her real name was Grace. I had a nickname, too.

Really? What was your nickname?

Meeley. Do you have a nickname?

No, but now I wish I did! Those are fun nicknames!

Do you want to make one up right now?

Okay! Let's see... how about Treasure Map?

Why would your nickname be Treasure Map?

Because there is an X in my name, and X marks the spot on a treasure map!

I like it! Good thinking, Treasure Map!

Thanks! So what did you and your sister Pidge do when you were kids?

We had a lot of fun going on adventures. I was always the leader.

I like going on adventures, too! One time I pretended I was digging up a dinosaur skeleton in my backyard.

That sounds fun. Pidge and I did activities like that.

We would explore our neighborhood every day. We would climb trees and collect bugs as pets.

I like playing outside. There are so many fun things to do, especially if you use your imagination.

I think so, too. Our mom was very supportive of our outdoor adventures.

Shouldn't moms always be supportive of their children?

Yes, but in that time in history, girls were not allowed to do all the fun things boys could do.

Like what?

For one thing, girls were always supposed to wear skirts and dresses. But our mom let us wear bloomers, which are like poofy pants.

Why were girls not allowed to wear pants?

People thought girls wearing pants was not "ladylike." But our mom wanted us to be independent.

My mom wants me to be independent, too!

That's a good mom. Sometimes society has prejudiced rules that you should ignore.

I agree! If you want to wear pants, then you should wear pants!

Exactly!

What was it like growing up in Kansas?

I didn't always live in Kansas. Because of my dad's job as a railroad worker, we moved around.

Where all did you live?

We moved to Des Moines, Iowa when I was nine and then I spent my high school years in Chicago, Illinois.

You grew up in three cities?!

Maybe all that traveling and moving made me want to travel even more.

That makes sense!

Wherever I was living, I kept a scrapbook of newspaper clippings that talked about women who were successful in jobs that men usually did.

Women didn't do all the jobs of men back then?

No. Women were not allowed to do many things, like vote.

Women couldn't vote?!

Yes, but that's a whole other conversation. If you were a woman in 1916, all you were expected to do was get married and have children.

Also...WOMEN COULDN'T VOTE?!?!

Women could not vote until 1920 in America.

But that's not that long ago in history!

Tell me about it.

So did you do what society wanted you to do?

No, I most certainly did not. I learned to fly airplanes.

That's so cool.

During my first flight on an airplane as a passenger, I was hooked. By the time I had gotten two or three hundred feet off the ground, I knew I had to fly.

Was it hard learning to fly?

It was very hard, and it was very expensive. I had to work several jobs to save enough to pay for the lessons. And my mom helped pay because she believed in me.

Did you pass the flying test?

I did! I was only the 16th woman in America to get a pilot's license.

Congrats!

Thanks! That was just the beginning of my aviation career. I started writing in newspapers saying how great flying was. I also flew long flights with other pilots, and the world started to know who I was.

Did you become famous?

Yes I did. And as my fame grew, I kept promoting aviation. Then in 1932, something very exciting happened.

Ooh! What happened?

I flew all alone, nonstop, across the Atlantic Ocean. I was the first woman ever to do that.

That's incredible!

I received several medals, and I even met the president!

Wow!

I continued flying for the rest of my life. I loved flying.

I love flying as a passenger on a plane. I can only imagine how fun it must be to pilot a plane!

It's the closest you can get to feeling like a bird. You get to control a machine that lets you fly through the air.

Society was not allowing me to do what I wanted, but up in the air, in that cockpit, I had control of my life.

You were setting your own course for greatness!

That's very good, Treasure Map!

Did other women start being pilots like you?

Yes. I actually was the first president of a group called The Ninety-Nines, which was an international group of female pilots.

I bet those meetings were fun! Imagine the far off places all of you traveled to!

Yes! The world has so many places to see and explore, Alex. You should explore everything you want. Don't let society tell you otherwise.

I won't!

Your whole life is a treasure map, and you get to find the treasures by exploring.

Then I think I picked the right nickname for me!

You sure did!

I have one more question for you.

Okay!

Do you think I should be an aviator when I grow up?

Becoming an aviator is very difficult. You need to train very hard and know math very well. But if you work hard like I did, you can be an aviator, too!

Thank you for the advice!

You're welcome!

It was fun talking to
Amelia Earhart!

I think I want to be an
aviator now.

But there are a lot more
aviators
I can text
to learn more.

I can't wait to text
the next one!

FUN QUESTIONS FOR YOU FROM . . .

AMELIA EARHART

WRITE YOUR ANSWERS IN THE TEXTING BUBBLES!

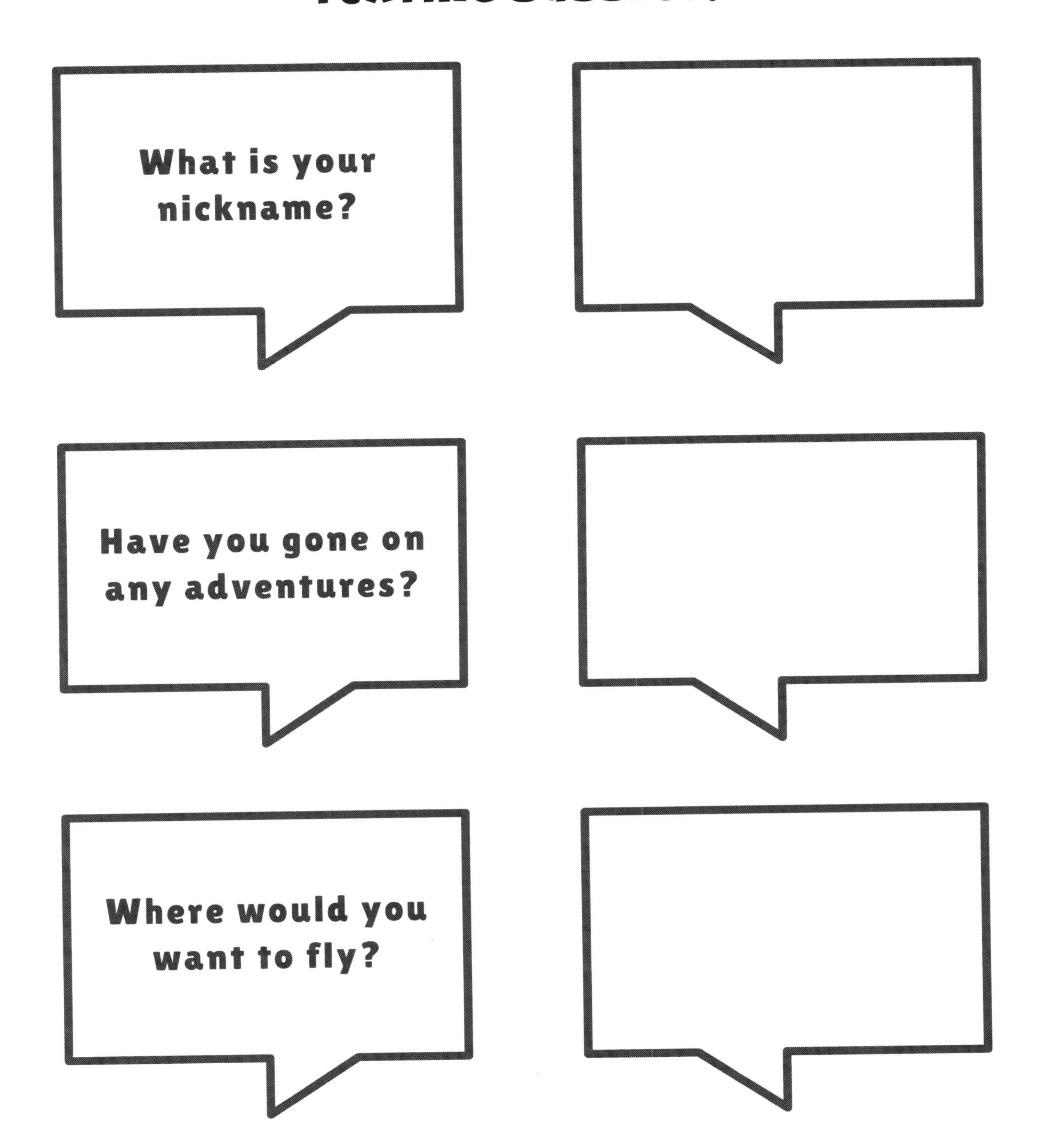

COMPARE AND CONTRAST WITH . . .
AMELIA EARHART

How are you and Amelia the same?

How are you and Amelia different?

THINKING ABOUT THE LIFE OF . . .

AMELIA EARHART

How did Amelia's life make you feel?

Would you want to live a day in Amelia's life? Why or why not?

LEARNING FROM . . .

AMELIA EARHART

What did you find most interesting about Amelia's life?

What did Amelia teach you?

WHAT FIVE W QUESTIONS WOULD YOU TEXT AMELIA EARHART?

1. Who ______________________________?

2. What ______________________________?

3. When ______________________________?

4. Where ______________________________?

5. Why ______________________________?

MEME TIME WITH . . .

AMELIA EARHART

DRAW A PICTURE THAT DESCRIBES AMELIA EARHARTS'S LIFE!

"Adventure is worthwhile in itself."

- Amelia Earhart

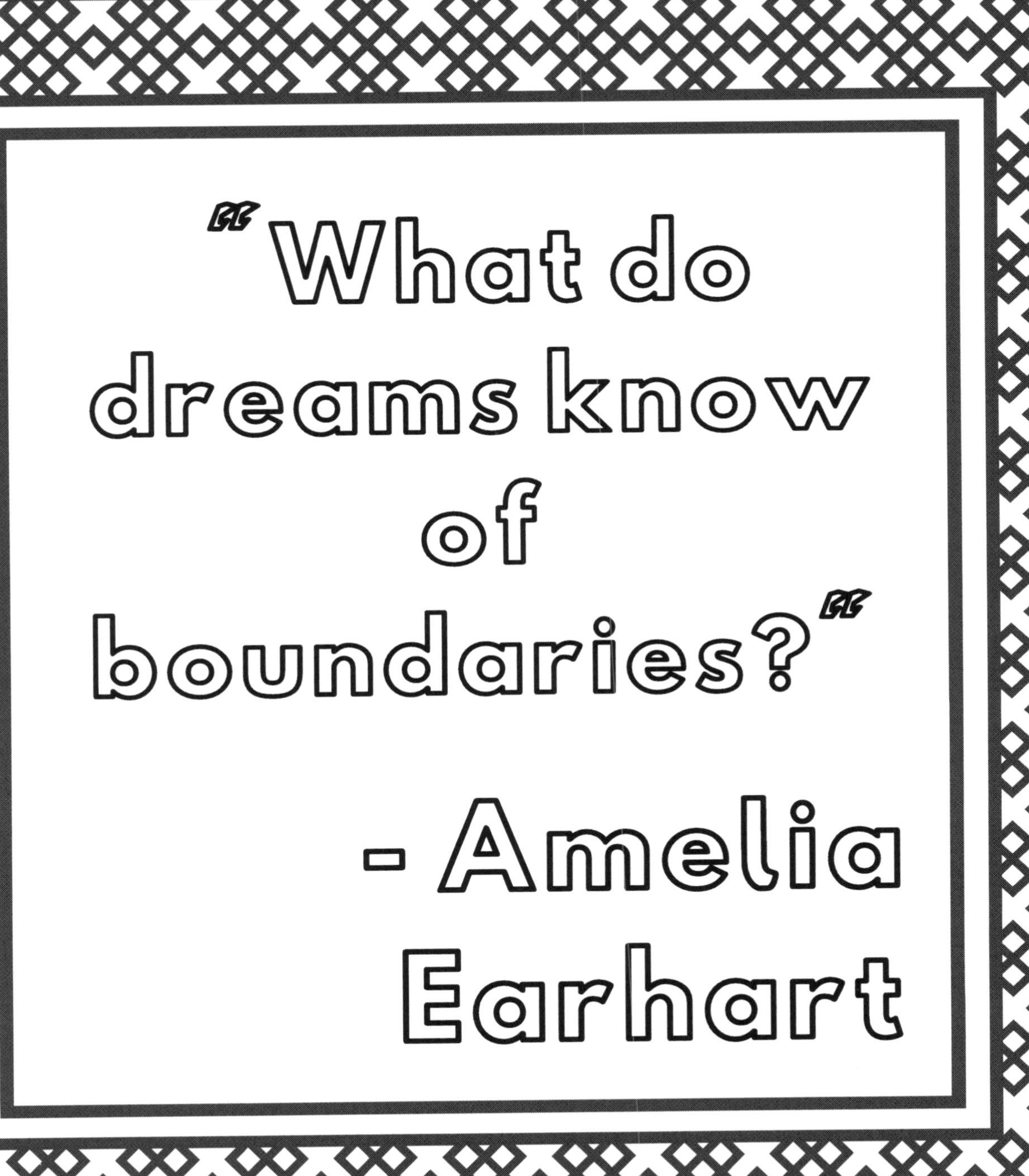
"What do dreams know of boundaries?"
- Amelia Earhart

“A single act of kindness throws out roots in all directions, and the roots spring up and make new trees.”

- Amelia Earhart

Texting with...

Harriet Tubman

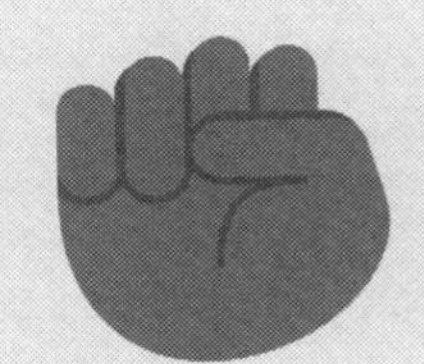

An Underground Railroad Black History Biography Book for Kids

Written by Bobby Basil

Hi! I'm Alex!

I’m nine, and I don't know
what I want to be
when I grow up.

There are so many
amazing things to do!

My mom helps me text with
important people and ask them
questions about their lives.

It's fun to ask questions!

Today
my mom and I are
texting with...

Harriet Tubman!

Harriet Tubman was a
social activist
that lived from 1822 until 1913.

She helped free
dozens of enslaved people
and fought for women's equality.

I can't wait to text her
my questions!

Hi
Harriet!

Hi Alex!

Thank you
for texting
with me.

You're
welcome.

What do
you look
like?

I look like
this...

Where were you born?

I was born in Dorchester County, Maryland.

What was your childhood like?

I had a very difficult childhood. I was born an enslaved person.

What is an enslaved person?

For hundreds of years in America, black people were treated like they were objects. They were bought and sold like they were animals. These human beings were enslaved by other human beings.

That's terrible!

It was.

Weren't there laws making slavery illegal?

Not for a long time. There were actually laws that said slavery was okay.

That doesn't make sense! Why would people think slavery is okay?

Many people in that time were racist against black people. They thought black people were not human beings.

Those people are stupid!

They aren't
stupid, Alex.
They are
ignorant.

What's the
difference?

Ignorance is when
someone doesn't
have the correct
information.

How could a
person not know
that all humans
are equal?
That's obvious!

Racism is taught.
It's passed down
from generation
to generation.

These ignorant people were taught by their parents that black people were bad.

Those are terrible parents! My mom would never teach me that!

That's good. No one should ever teach hate. We all deserve to be treated with respect.

What was it like being an enslaved person?

My owners forced me to work as a child, and they hurt me if they were not pleased.

I'm really sorry. That's awful.

I appreciate that. I learned from my mother that you could fight back and resist. In 1849, I escaped from slavery. I walked ninety miles on foot.

That's a really long way to walk.

It was. And it was very dangerous because I could have been caught at any moment.

Did anyone help you as you escaped?

Yes. I received help through the Underground Railroad.

What's the Underground Railroad?

It was a network of secret routes and safe hideouts for escaped enslaved people to use.

It stretched from the southern states of America all the way up to Canada in the north.

So it didn't have anything to do with trains?

It did. Like the railroad, each safe place enslaved people stayed was called a "station." And each person who helped along the way was called a "conductor."

So the conductors were transporting enslaved people like railroads transported cargo?

Exactly. Except these conductors were transporting enslaved people to freedom. I had to travel by night to avoid being captured. I followed the North Star in the sky to help guide me to the north, where slavery was illegal.

Did you make it?

I did!

Yay!!!

I made it to Pennsylvania, which was a free state.

When I found I had crossed that line into the north, I felt like I was in Heaven. Then I thought of something sad.

What was it?

I thought of how the rest of my family were still not free.

That is sad.

I decided to go back to the south and help free my family.

I wouldn't want my family to stay slaves, either. I love my family, even though sometimes they make me angry.

Family is very important, and standing up for your family is one way of showing that you love them. After I helped free my family, I went back to free more enslaved people.

You were like a superhero! You helped so many people!

I did, but it wasn't just me.

It was all the people along the Underground Railroad that helped. Many people risked their lives to help enslaved people get to freedom. I rescued seventy enslaved people over thirteen trips. I also helped dozens of others with instructions on how to escape.

I don't know if I would have had the courage to do what you did.

I knew it was the right thing to do, and that's what gave me courage.

What did you do after the Underground Railroad?

I helped the northern side in the Civil War end slavery. I took care of soldiers as a nurse and I was a spy.

You were a spy?!

Yes. I would wear the enemy's uniform and scout good locations to attack. I also was the first woman to lead a battle in the Civil War.

Wow! You are an incredible person!

Thank you, Alex. I rescued 750 enslaved people in that battle.

I once stood up to a bully in school. He was picking on my friend Katie. But that's not as important as rescuing 750 enslaved people.

It is as important, Alex. Because you helped another human being. Every good deed you do for someone else is important, no matter how small.

I guess you're right... Did your side win the Civil War?

We did! And the government passed laws that ended slavery.

That's awesome! Did the war end racism, too?

Sadly, it did not. Many people are still racist, even in your time.

Even after fighting a war and everything?

Even then.

Why are there still ignorant people in the world?

They don't have the knowledge they need.

In my time, people also were ignorant about women's rights. They thought women should not get to vote.

You gotta be KIDDING me!

It's true. That was another wrong I fought against. After the Civil War, I gave speeches in America saying women should have the right to vote.

You did so many great things in your life. How can I ever be as great as you?

Don't compare yourself to others, Alex. We all have something special about us that no one else has. Let your special light shine for the world.

Thank you for the advice!

You’re welcome!

It was fun talking to
Harriet Tubman!

I think I want to be a
social activist now.

But there are a lot more
social activists
I can text
to learn more.

I can't wait to text
the next one!

FUN QUESTIONS FOR YOU FROM . . .

HARRIET TUBMAN

WRITE YOUR ANSWERS IN THE TEXTING BUBBLES!

What is your special light that shines for the world?

How have you stood up for yourself and what you believe?

What is a good deed you have done for someone else?

COMPARE AND CONTRAST WITH . . .

HARRIET TUBMAN

How are you and Harriet the same?

____

____

____

____

How are you and Harriet different?

____

____

____

____

THINKING ABOUT THE LIFE OF . . .

HARRIET TUBMAN

How did Harriet's life make you feel?

Would you want to live a day in Harriet's life? Why or why not?

LEARNING FROM . . .

HARRIET TUBMAN

What did you find most interesting about Harriet's life?

What did Harriet teach you?

WHAT FIVE W QUESTIONS WOULD YOU TEXT

HARRIET TUBMAN?

1. **Who** ______________________________ **?**

2. **What** ______________________________ **?**

3. **When** ______________________________ **?**

4. **Where** ______________________________ **?**

5. **Why** ______________________________ **?**

Meme Time with . . .

HARRIET TUBMAN

Draw a picture that describes Harriet Tubman's life!

"Every great dream begins with a dreamer."

- Harriet Tubman

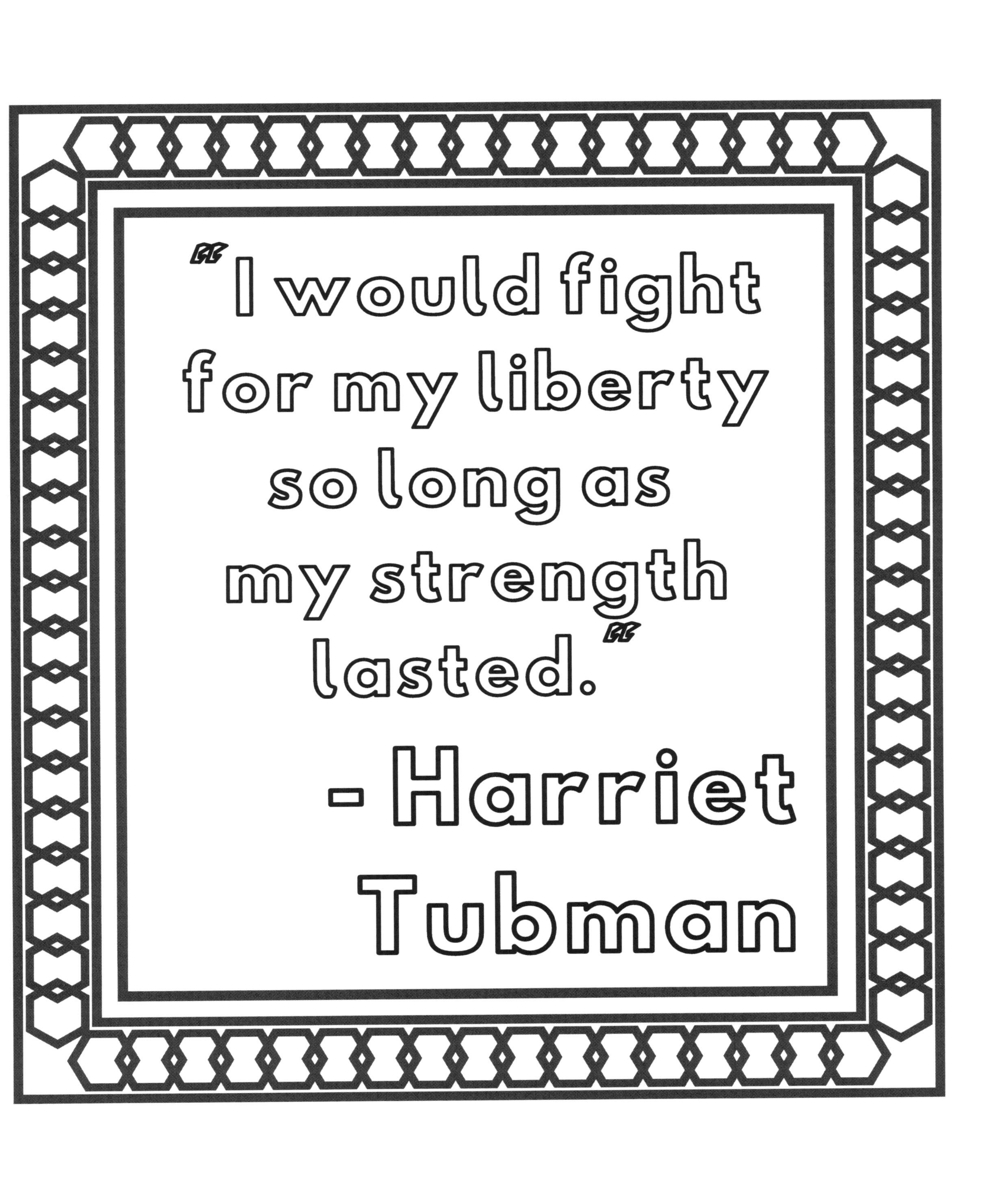
"I would fight for my liberty so long as my strength lasted."
- Harriet Tubman

"If you want a taste of freedom, keep going."

- Harriet Tubman

Texting with...

An Ancient Egypt Biography Book for Kids

Written by Bobby Basil

Hi! I'm Alex!

I’m nine, and I don't know
what I want to be
when I grow up.

There are so many
amazing things to do!

My mom helps me text with
important people and ask them
questions about their lives.

It's fun to ask questions!

Today
my mom and I are
texting with...

Cleopatra!

Cleopatra was a
ruler of Ancient Egypt
that lived from 69 BC until 30 BC.

She was the
last ruler of Egypt before the
Roman Empire.

I can't wait to text her
my questions!

Hi Cleopatra!

Hi Alex!

Thank you for texting with me.

You're welcome.

What do you look like?

I look like this...

Where were you born?

I was born in Alexandria, which was in the Ptolemaic Kingdom.

I've never heard of the Ptolemaic Kingdom before.

It was a kingdom that started from Ancient Greece.

When I was born, the center of the kingdom was in Egypt.

Ooh! So you grew up in Ancient Egypt? Did you live with mummies and sleep in tombs and stuff?

No, Alex. I think you may have been getting some wrong information. We did have mummies, but our civilization was very advanced.

So you never slept in a tomb?

No.

That's too bad. They're so spooky!

I actually slept in a palace, because I was the Pharoah of Egypt.

Is a Pharoah like a princess?

It's better than a princess. As Pharoah, I was like a queen and ruled over everything. My family was royalty, so I was raised with many opportunities other people did not have.

Like what?

For one, I had my own tutor as a child who taught me about philosophy. And I got to study at the Library of Alexandria.

That's almost my name!

You're right!

I love going to the library. I have my own library card. My mom lets me check out as many books as I can carry. I should call it the Library of Me!

This was one of the largest libraries in the world.

The Library of Alexandria had up to 400,000 scrolls you could read.

You didn't have books back then?

Books like the kind you check out from the library weren't invented until 1440. Before then, people had to write everything by hand.

That must have taken a long time!

It did. And I got to read all of it!

I learned at least ten languages. And I was the first of my family to learn Egyptian.

Why didn't your family learn Egyptian? Didn't they live in Egypt?

They did not have to learn it because all of the powerful people spoke Greek.

That's cool you were trying to fit in with the people in your kingdom!

I wanted to bring many countries together.

A good way to do that was by learning many languages.

I want to learn ten languages like you.

It's very good to know more than just one language. You can use it when you travel or to make a new friend.

My friend Pete has a friend named Pedro. Pedro speaks Spanish. I wish I spoke Spanish so we could talk at lunch.

I bet Pedro would love to teach you Spanish, and you could teach him English!

I like that idea! So when did you become Pharoah?

When I was only seventeen years old. I had a lot of problems to fix as soon as I became Pharoah. There was a drought in Egypt and many people were hungry.

What did you do?

I ordered that my government give hungry people food.

That's a nice thing to do!

There were problems like that all the time when I was Pharoah. But a big problem was my brother wanted to rule Egypt.

Uh oh. Big problem.

It was. My brother and I fought over who would get to rule Egypt.

Who won?

A famous Roman, Julius Caesar, said we should call a truce and be okay sharing the throne.

How come that guy got to say what happened?

He was trying to take over Egypt and had a large and powerful army. We had to listen to him. As Caesar grew more powerful, he let me rule Egypt on my own.

Why did he do that?

He liked me.

So did you get to rule Egypt forever?

No. This was a time in history when the Roman Empire was started. Julius Caesar became the emperor of Rome.

Is that like a Pharoah?

Yes. Except the Roman Empire was much larger than Egypt. Caesar was more powerful than anyone else on earth.

It's good he liked you!

Yes, except many other people wanted his power, so he died.

Oh no!

Power is a strange thing, Alex. People will do very bad things to get it.

That reminds me of Lloyd. He ran for class president, but he was mean about it.

What do you mean?

He said the person he was running against, Jill, snored in her sleep. How would he even know that?!

He spread a rumor?

He did!

Did Lloyd win the election?

No. I went around the school and had students sign something that said Lloyd was lying, and the teachers kicked him out of the election.

That's very smart.

People shouldn't try and become powerful by lying and cheating.

In my time, people did much worse things than lie and cheat to get the thrown of power.

That's not nice.

You're right. After Julius Caesar, more men fought over Egypt. In the end, Octavian the Roman emperor won and made Egypt part of Rome.

I was the last Pharoah to rule Egypt.

I don't think I would want to be a Pharoah.

Why not?

It sounds like you don't have job security. Anyone could take the job away from you!

That's true.

Also, my mom's not a queen, so I don't think I could ever be a Pharoah. But I think I'm going to run for class president next year. I liked talking to people when they signed that sheet for me.

I think you would be a fantastic president. As long as you are fair and decent to the people you represent, then you will do well.

Thank you for the advice!

You're welcome!

It was fun talking to
Cleopatra!

I think I want to
learn more about Ancient Egypt
and Ancient Rome now.

There are a lot more people
from then
that I can text
to learn more.

I can't wait to text
the next one!

FUN QUESTIONS FOR YOU FROM . . .

CLEOPATRA

WRITE YOUR ANSWERS IN THE TEXTING BUBBLES!

COMPARE AND CONTRAST WITH . . .
CLEOPATRA

How are you and Cleopatra the same?

____

____

____

____

How are you and Cleopatra different?

____

____

____

____

THINKING ABOUT THE LIFE OF . . .

CLEOPATRA

How did Cleopatra's life make you feel?

____

____

____

____

Would you want to live a day in Cleopatra's life?
Why or why not?

____

____

____

____

LEARNING FROM . . .
CLEOPATRA

What did you find most interesting about Cleopatra's life?

What did Cleopatra teach you?

WHAT FIVE W QUESTIONS WOULD YOU TEXT CLEOPATRA?

1. Who ____?

2. What ____?

3. When ____?

4. Where ____?

5. Why ____?

Meme Time with . . .

Cleopatra

Draw a picture that describes Cleopatra's life!

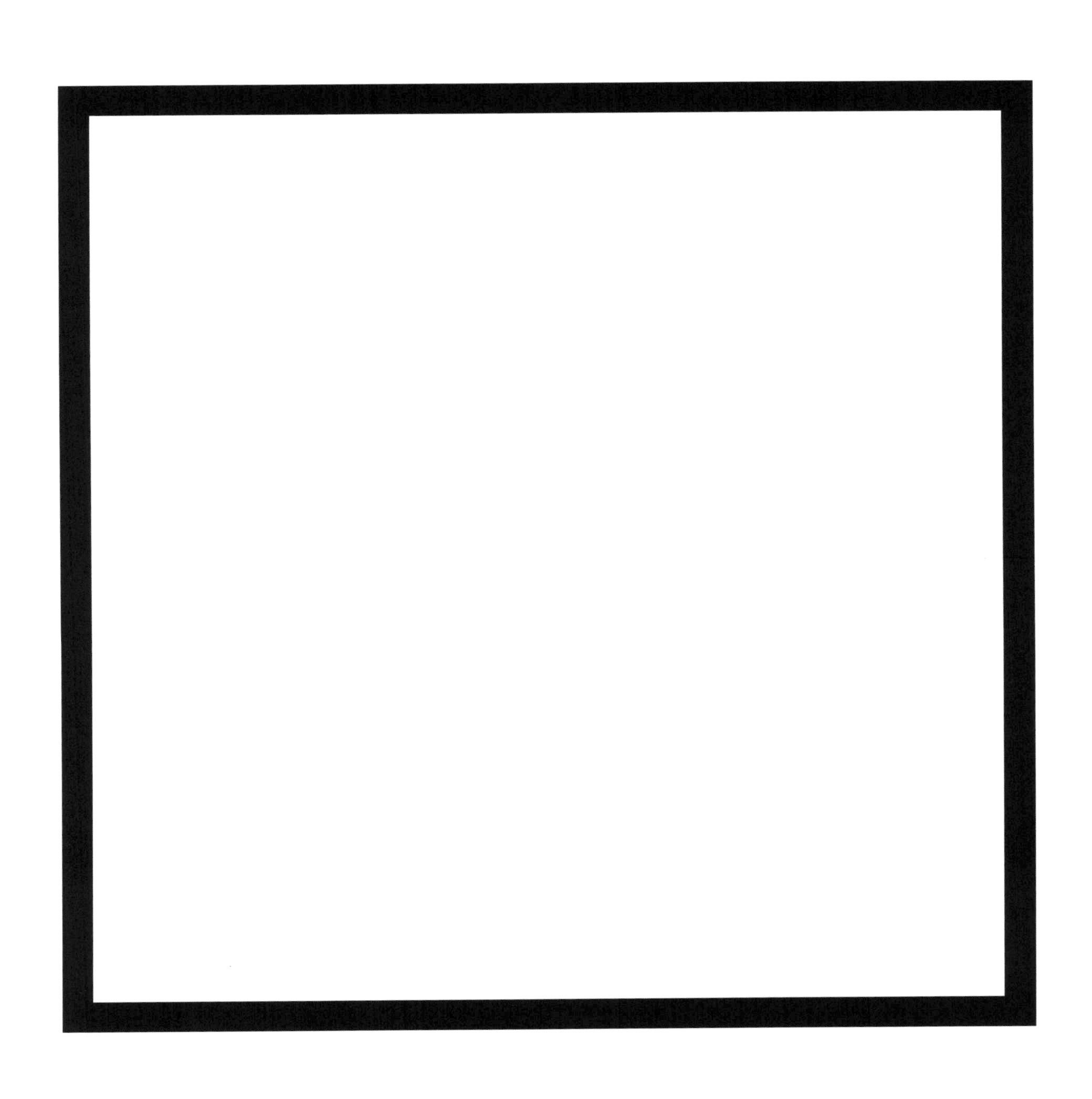

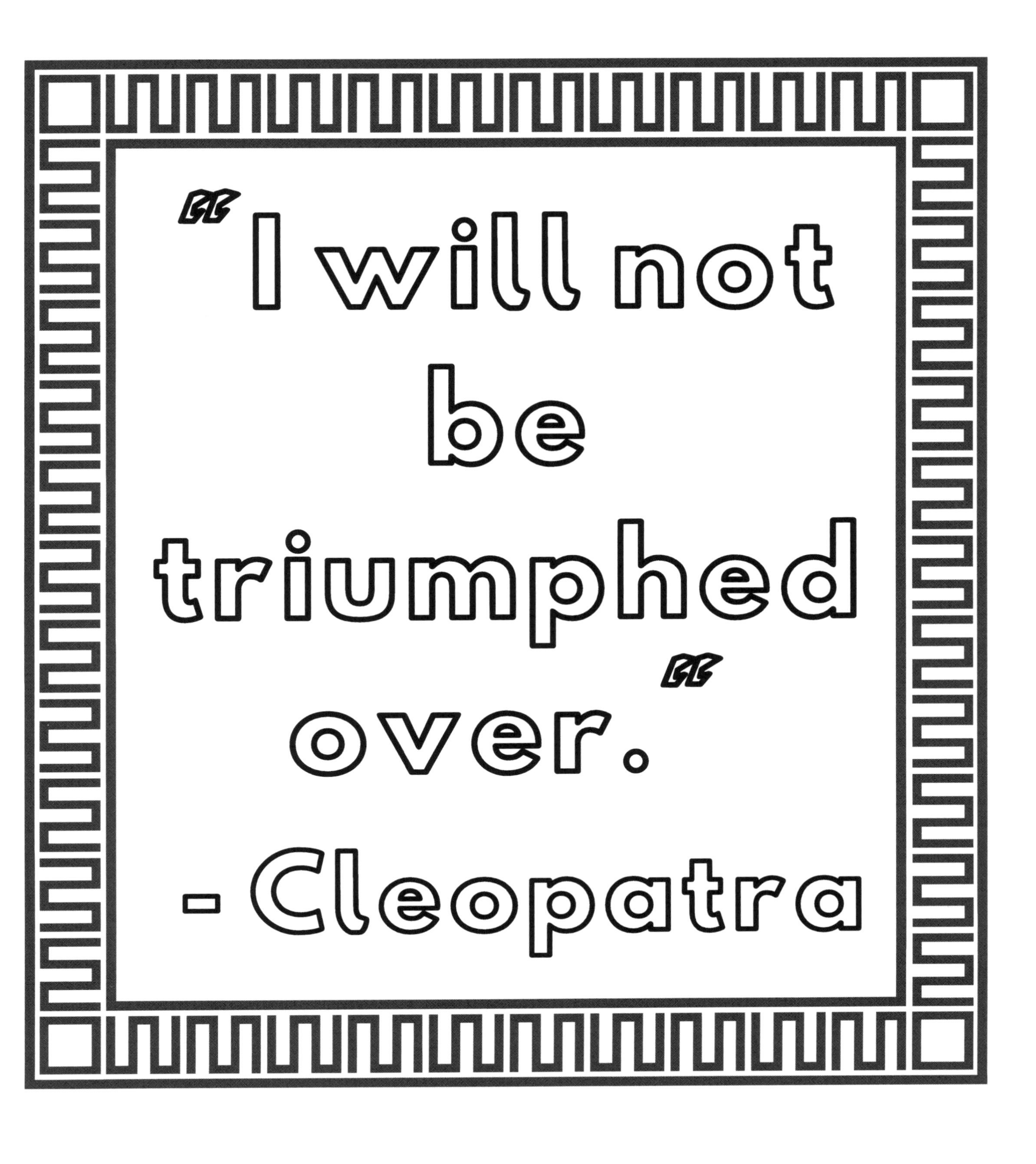
"I will not
be
triumphed
over."
- Cleopatra

"Be it known that we, the greatest, are misthought."

- Cleopatra

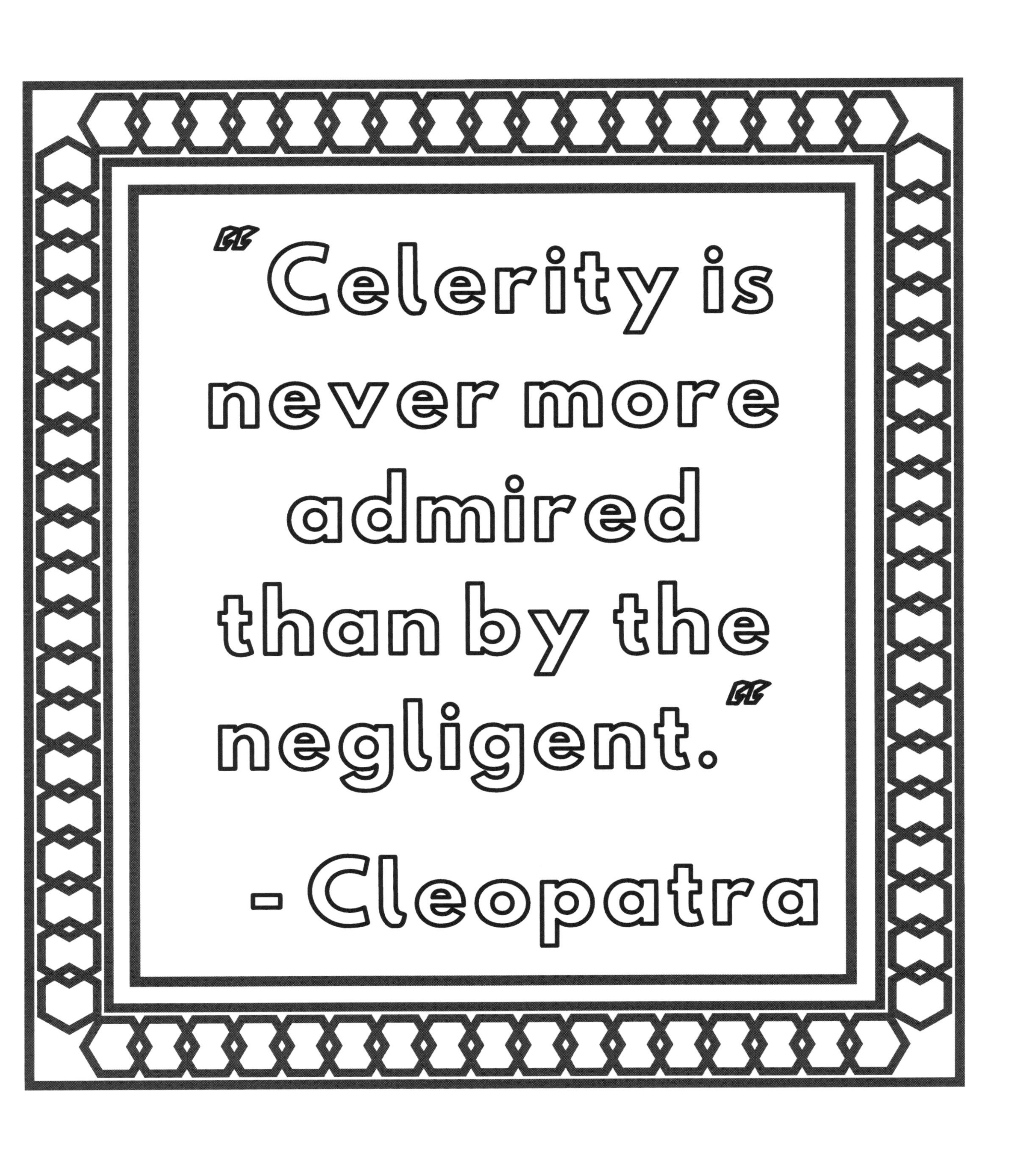
"Celerity is never more admired than by the negligent."
- Cleopatra

Your review will help other readers discover my books.

Thank you!

Made in the USA
Middletown, DE
19 October 2020

22351381R00066